# SCOTLAND

First published in Great Britain in 1994 by
Colin Baxter Photography Ltd
Grantown-on-Spey,
Moray, PH26 3NA
Scotland

Reprinted in Paperback in 1995, 1998
Revised edition 2001

A CIP catalogue record for this book is available from the British Library

ISBN 1-84107-114-5

Text copyright © Iseabail Macleod 1994, 2001
Design by Zoë Hall, Studio Z, Edinburgh
Printed in Hong Kong

Front Cover Photograph CASTLE STALKER AND LISMORE, ARGYLL
Back Cover Photograph IONA POST OFFICE

# SCOTLAND

Photographs by
## Colin Baxter

Colin Baxter Photography, Grantown-on-Spey, Scotland

# INTRODUCTION

There are very few countries that have such a wide variety of beautiful scenery within such a small place as Scotland. Its heavily indented western seaboard and numerous islands, large and small, off the western and northern coasts, give it an extraordinarily long coastline and ensure that no part of Scotland is more than 40 or 50 miles (64 or 80 km) from the sea. It is generally thought of as being divided into the Highlands in the north and Lowlands in the south, but this north-south division is not as simple as it seems. A glance at a physical map will show that most of the flatter land is towards the east, rather than the south, and this is where Scotland's rich farming country is to be found, from the plains of the south-east, northwards through Fife to Angus, Buchan and beyond. Even as far north as Caithness, flat plains on the east give way to rugged hills in the west.

The climate too varies, from milder but wetter conditions in the west to the drier weather of the east. Vegetation is influenced by these factors and although the east is more fertile, climatic conditions in the west produce, in some areas, a lushness of flowers and shrubs which give unexpected pleasure to many visitors to these latitudes. Introduced azalea and rhododendron grow well in the peaty soil, and the latter are now often found wild, and indeed create a problem for native plants. In late summer the hills and moors are bright with the purple of the heather, and the occasional splash of red from the berries of

the rowan. Much of Scotland was once covered with forests, especially of Caledonian pine; only remnants of this are to be seen throughout the Highlands, notably in the area around the Cairngorm mountains. Fine old oak trees are also found as well as birch, hazel and alder and other native species. Most other trees have been introduced, including larch from the early eighteenth century, which now forms large areas of bright colour in early spring and autumn. Since the First World War there has been an extensive afforestation programme, concentrating on fast-growing but less aesthetic species, notably the Sitka spruce from North America, which now stretches in serried ranks over so many hillsides. These forests are fenced off from the red deer, originally a forest animal, but since the destruction of Scotland's natural woodland, it has adapted to the open hill and moor. Visitors have on occasion suffered disappointment on finding that an area designated as 'Forest of…' is a stretch of a bare hill or moor, with not a tree in sight.

Deer-hunting has always been a popular sport in Scotland and medieval royal hunting lodges still survive, even if only in ruined form. In the nineteenth century, this profitable sport was developed by the landlords, and it continues to be a source of income in the Highlands. The social cost was however high and, along with large-scale sheep farming, it was one of the main causes of the Highland Clearances, when large numbers of the local population in the Highlands and Islands were removed from their crofts by the landlords to make way for these activities. Others were more voluntary emigrants from the hard conditions of crofting life, and their descendants are today scattered throughout the globe, many of them now returning to search for their roots. Those who did not emigrate were often forced to move from the countryside into the rapidly growing towns and cities. Increasingly, town-dwellers have returned to the country for recreation, using many of Scotland's unique landscapes in new and creative ways.

Thus skiing and mountaineering are enjoyed by many people, the former having been developed on a commercial basis since the 1960s. Hill-walking has become more and more popular in recent times. Scotland's mountains have been classified over the years into various height categories, including 'Munros' at 3,000 feet (914 metres) or over. 'Munro-bagging', aiming to climb all 280-odd of these, has become a prevalent and somewhat competitive pastime. For the more ambitious mountaineer, Scotland's mountains offer spectacular climbs, especially in winter, which often surprises those accustomed to the grander heights of the Alps and other mountains, where 3,000 feet is a mere foothill. Probably the most challenging are the Cuillin Hills in the Isle of Skye. Scotland's highest mountain is however Ben Nevis, near Fort William, and the area has many splendid climbs, as well as a ski development on Aonach Mòr, just to the east. Another popular skiing area is the Cairngorms, in the central Highlands, which contains four of Scotland's highest mountains, and forms one of Britain's largest National Nature Reserves.

In the modern world there is an increasing need for conservation and protection of landscape and habitats, and a great deal has been done in Scotland to this end. Much of this important work is carried out by Scottish Natural Heritage, formed in 1992 from the Countryside Commission and the Nature Conservancy Council, and covering National Scenic Areas and Sites of Special Scientific Interest, as well as Nature Reserves. These areas cover large tracts of the country and contain some of Scotland's grandest scenery. The National Nature Reserves also include, for example, Inverpolly, which takes in a vast area of mountain, loch and coast in the far north-west; Ben Eighe, a little further south, with striking mountain scenery and natural woodland; and the small island of Rum off the west coast, with steep craggy mountains sweeping straight down to the sea in a way which is characteristically Scottish. Indeed much of Scotland's scenery is dominated by water; 'loch' refers not only to the numerous freshwater lakes but also to the coastal fjords or arms of the sea, which form such a large part of the lengthy western coastline. Rivers often rise as turbulent streams in narrow glens, flowing down to the flatter straths and plains below. Myriads of islands, off the coast and in lochs and rivers, provide unique habitats for plants and wildlife.

★    ★    ★

Scotland's place-names are a mirror of her varied past, with mixtures of Celtic and Germanic, often misinterpreted in various ways over the centuries, leaving many puzzles for the place-name scholar. Gaelic names abound; the Gaelic-speaking Scots ruled

Scotland in the early Middle Ages and Gaelic place-names are found throughout the country, but intermingled with names in English, or Scots, as the English of Scotland came to be called by the sixteenth century. Other Celtic names include those from the language of the Britons, which was akin to modern Welsh. The Picts, who spoke a related language, also left their mark, especially in names beginning with *pit-*, such as Pitlochry, Pittenweem. Old Norse names are dominant in the Shetland and Orkney Islands which have populations of mainly Norse origin, but Norse names are often found in large numbers in the Western Isles and along the western seaboard, sometimes in Gaelicized form, as in Mallaig, Uig (from Old Norse *vík* a bay). These are reminders of the Viking invasions of the north and west of Scotland from the ninth to the thirteenth centuries. Problems with pronunciation frequently arise because of the difference in structure of the languages. In the Germanic languages the describing element comes first followed by the naming element, in the Celtic the other way round. Thus Gaelic 'beinn an *eòin*', mountain of the bird, would become in English '*bird* mountain'; in each case the stress falls on the describing element.

Possibly this mixture of peoples and the power struggles between them had some influence on the strongly defensive character of Scottish architecture, lasting long after the need for it had gone. Scotland abounds in castles, though few of the structures of her warring medieval past survive intact. The Scottish tower house was an elegantly grim fortress designed first and foremost to protect against enemies, its shape often enlivened by crowstep gables and pepperpot turrets, forming a style which later became known as Scottish baronial. Such castles continued to be built well into the seventeenth century when modern artillery had already rendered their defensive qualities obsolete. The style was revived in the nineteenth century, not only in the restoration of these old buildings, but in the creation of new ones, the numerous castles of the Romantic period, with ornate developments of the style, sometimes bordering on the absurd. The royal castle of Balmoral is a classic example, but they were built also for lords and lairds, for shipping magnates, engineering tycoons and merchant bankers, the rich and mighty of the Victorian period of expansion in industry and commerce. Some of the castles, however, which decorate the Scottish landscape today are pure restorations, replicas of their original medieval shapes, with few of the frills in which the nineteenth century delighted.

In the Middle Ages, there was considerable need for defence. When the direct line of the Gaelic monarchy died out in the late thirteenth century, the country was faced not only with dynastic struggles, but with a tussle for independence from her southern neighbour, and although a victory was won at the Battle of Bannockburn under King Robert the Bruce in 1314, these struggles continued at one level or another for centuries. In 1503, in an attempt to improve relations, King James IV married Margaret Tudor, a sister of Henry VIII. When Queen Elizabeth of England died in 1603, she was succeeded by their great-grandson, King James VI, who also became James I of England and Ireland. In 1688 the reigning Stewart monarch James VII and II, was deposed and exiled. In 1707, in the reign of his daughter, Queen Anne, the parliaments of the two countries were joined to form the new United Kingdom of Great Britain. In 1714 Queen Anne died childless and was succeeded by a German prince, a descendant of King James VI, who ruled as George I. Several Jacobite risings attempted to restore the Stewart kings (or Stuart as they were now called) in the person of James Francis Edward Stuart, known as the 'Old Pretender'. But hopes were finally dashed by the defeat of his son Prince Charles Edward Stuart ('Bonnie Prince Charlie') at Culloden, near Inverness, in April 1746.

As the century wore on it was expected in many quarters that the ways of life of the two countries would gradually converge. Culture north of the Border has however remained Scottish to this day, in language and literature and in many other ways. A strong survival of traditional music, both Highland and Lowland, is now valued well beyond these shores. The three areas of Scottish life which were specifically maintained by the Treaty of Union of 1707 were the legal and educational systems and the Church of Scotland as the established church. The role of religion in Scottish history has been diverse and intense. A Celtic form of Christianity, brought from Ireland by St Columba in the sixth century, later gave way to the church of Rome, which held sway until the Scottish Reformation in 1560. A few structures survive from pre-Reformation times, including the recently restored Abbey of Iona, built on the site of St Columba's church. In recent centuries, religious history has been one of strife, schism and, in some cases, reunification; quite small villages have been known to have three or more churches. Some areas, especially in the Western Isles and on the west coast, remained Roman Catholic, and the Catholic population was greatly increased in the nineteenth century by the immigration of large numbers of Irish, and smaller ones of Italians and others. The population has been further diversified by other immigrants, to form a modern multicultural Scotland.

Its distinctive identity is however by no means diminished. In 1997 there was an overwhelming vote for a new Scottish parliament, within the UK, which was inaugurated in 1999.

The landscape too has seen change, with industrialization, developments in agriculture and other alterations in land use. But the mountains and glens, lochs and rivers remain, along with the stunningly beautiful coastline, with reminders here and there of Scotland's stormy past. Colin Baxter's photographs help us to appreciate Scotland's landscapes in a new way: light and shade, sunshine and mist, and the ever-changing colours which create the infinite variety in this part of northern Europe.

*Iseabail Macleod*

*GLENFINNAN VIADUCT, WEST HIGHLAND LINE*
*At one time steam was the main means of bringing visitors into Scotland's*
*magnificent west Highland scenery. Though now replaced by the car and the diesel train,*
*steam trains have recently been re-introduced as a tourist attraction. In past centuries, transport*
*was easiest by water, which was one of the reasons why it was at the head of the long*
*freshwater Loch Shiel, opposite, that Prince Charles Edward Stuart raised his*
*standard on 19 August 1745, at the start of the last Jacobite rising.*

*ORONSAY, LOCH BRACADALE, ISLE OF SKYE*
*There are several 'Oronsays' (with one spelling or another) in the Western Isles,*
*all from Old Norse 'orfiris ey' meaning ebb island; most of them can be reached*
*on foot at low tide.*

*THE RIVER GARRY AT KILLIECRANKIE, PERTHSHIRE*

*LOCH SCRIDAIN AND BEN MORE, ISLE OF MULL*

16

*LOCH TUATH AND GOMETRA, ISLE OF MULL*
*Loch Tuath, 'north loch', is the strait separating Mull from two*
*neighbouring islands, Gometra and the much larger Ulva. Ben More, opposite,*
*from Gaelic, 'beinn mhòr', meaning big hill, is predictably a common hill name in the north.*
*Mull's Ben More deserves the name, being the highest island*
*mountain outside the Cuillins of Skye.*

*ARISAIG POST OFFICE, INVERNESS-SHIRE*
*The bays around Arisaig look towards the craggy mountains of Rum*
*and to the smoother basalt cliffs of Eigg, opposite. White sands are a spectacular*
*feature of the coast between Arisaig and Morar.*

*EIGG AND RUM FROM NEAR ARISAIG*

*CARRBRIDGE, STRATHSPEY*
*The ancient bridge over the River Dulnain, in the village of*
*Carrbridge, was built in 1717 to make the river crossing easier for*
*funerals. Opposite: The plateau of the nearby Cairngorm mountains is*
*one of the wildest areas in the British Isles. Its winter conditions*
*are frequently arctic, creating great danger for*
*the unwary.*

WHITEN HEAD FROM CEANNABEINNE, NEAR DURNESS

*Along the rugged northern coastline of Sutherland, beautiful
sandy bays alternate with complicated rock structures, where the sea
has hollowed out numerous spectacular caves. The famous
Smoo Cave is a few miles to the north-west.*

*WHITEN HEAD FROM THE BEACH AT CEANNABEINNE*
*From the rocky shore, the cliffs of Whiten Head rise starkly*
*in the distance, across the mouth of Loch Eriboll. Sunlight catches their*
*pale colour, making clear the origin of the name (in Gaelic,*
*'An Ceann Geal' the white head).*

CASTLE STALKER, APPIN, ARGYLL

*This square tower, on a tiny island just off the shores*
*of Loch Laich, dates from the reign of James IV, who used it as a*
*hunting lodge. It was restored in the nineteenth century. Opposite: The Castle*
*looks across to the fertile island of Lismore, the seat of the bishops of*
*Argyll from the twelfth century until the Reformation.*

*CASTLE STALKER AND LISMORE, ARGYLL*

*ARDTRECK POINT AND ORONSAY, ISLE OF SKYE*

*THE TROSSACHS AND LOCH KATRINE*

LAMMERMUIR HILLS

*The Lammermuirs rise in gentle curves above the fertile*
*farmlands of the south-east. Opposite: Hundleshope Heights are part of*
*the Southern Uplands Hills, which almost encircle Peebles,*
*and stretch south into the Borders.*

ST KILDA

*The most westerly group of Scottish islands, with their large colonies*
*of seabirds, lie 40 miles to the west of Harris. The main island, Hirta, has*
*the highest sea cliff in the British Isles. Until 1930 it supported a small community,*
*and the abandoned village has been partly restored. In 1987 St Kilda*
*became Scotland's first World Heritage Site. The beautiful and*
*usually inaccessible Soay, opposite, lies to the north-west.*

*DUART CASTLE, ISLE OF MULL*
*Seat of the chiefs of Clan Maclean, Duart Castle stands high*
*above Duart Bay on the east coast of Mull, and can be clearly seen from the*
*Oban–Craignure ferry as it approaches Mull. The medieval ruin*
*was restored in the nineteenth century.*

### TOBERMORY, ISLE OF MULL

*One of the most attractive towns on the west coast, Tobermory
is a popular anchorage for yachts. In midsummer its harbour is bright
with colourful boats and sails, especially in mid July, when it is the goal
of the Clyde Cruising Club's Tobermory Race, and during
West Highland Week in early August.*

*LOCH SHIELDAIG, WESTER ROSS*
*The name comes from Old Norse 'síld-vík' meaning herring bay.*
*The attractive little village of Shieldaig nestles on its shores below Ben*
*Shieldaig. Opposite: Ben Alligin, on the other side of Loch*
*Torridon, looms in dark cloud.*

*BROUGHTON HEIGHTS, BORDERS*
*Snow and frost add sparkle to the Broughton Heights,*
*which rise above the village of Broughton, between Peebles and Biggar.*
*The Border Country is steeped in history and romance and these were strong*
*influences on the young John Buchan when he spent summers visiting*
*his grandparents in Broughton.*

*INCHCAILLOCH, LOCH LOMOND*

*LOCH PORTREE AND THE CUILLIN HILLS, ISLE OF SKYE*
*The Cuillin Hills grace many a distant view on Skye.*
*Their highest summit, Sgurr Alasdair, is named after the nineteenth century*
*Gaelic scholar and climbing pioneer, Sheriff Alexander Nicolson.*

PORTREE HARBOUR, ISLE OF SKYE

*Portree is the main town on Skye. The name is from Gaelic 'Port an Righ'*
*port of the king, said to derive from a visit of King James V in 1540.*

BLAIR CASTLE AND CÀRN LIATH, PERTHSHIRE

*A fairy-tale medieval castle belonging to the Duke of Atholl, it was
restored in the nineteenth century. Gleaming white walls are echoed by a film
of frost and snow. Càrn Liath, on the right, means
'pale grey hill' in Gaelic.*

*POST BOX, GLEN ERROCHTY, PERTHSHIRE*

41

FALLS OF DOCHART, KILLIN, PERTHSHIRE

BEINN NA-H-EAGLAISE, TORRIDON, WESTER ROSS
*Torridon hills across Upper Loch Torridon, from the top of the Diabaig road.*

SANDWOOD BAY, SUTHERLAND

BEN LOYAL, SUTHERLAND
*Ben Loyal overlooks the Kyle of Tongue on the north coast.*

THE WALLACE MONUMENT, NEAR STIRLING

*Towering high against the backdrop of the Ochil Hills, this unusual
landmark commemorates Sir William Wallace, one of Scotland's great heroes,
who fought and died for his country in the Wars of Independence
in the early fourteenth century.*

*STIRLING CASTLE*
*Like Edinburgh, Stirling is built around a natural strong point*
*on a volcanic rock, and the Castle was an important royal residence for*
*the Stewart kings. The sixteenth-century royal palace has a*
*splendid Renaissance great hall.*

*THE SUMMER ISLES, WESTER ROSS*

*THE UPPER CLYDE VALLEY, LANARKSHIRE*

LOCH CARRON AND THE ISLE OF SKYE

*The calm waters of Loch Carron look towards the Red Hills in Skye.*
*Opposite: Looking across Loch Kishorn to Loch Carron. It is hard to believe*
*that the railway from Inverness runs along its precipitous shores, on*
*its way to nearby Plockton and to Kyle of Lochalsh.*

*LOCH MORLICH, STRATHSPEY*

*ABERNETHY FOREST AND LOCH GARTEN, STRATHSPEY*

*FADED TELEPHONE BOX, ISLE OF BARRA*

*SOUND OF IONA*
*The bold granite headlands of south-west Mull make a*
*contrast with a vivid blue sea.*

GLENCOE

*Weather conditions often give a sinister aspect to Glencoe,*
*remembered in Scotland as the scene of a massacre in February 1692,*
*when Government soldiers treacherously murdered local Macdonald inhabitants*
*with whom they had been billeted. The event was part of the efforts*
*of William of Orange to intimidate the Highland clans*
*still loyal to the deposed Stewart king.*

*LOCH ACHTRIOCHTAN, GLENCOE*

*DUNGAVEL HILL, LANARKSHIRE*

*NEAR WISTON, LANARKSHIRE*

*LOCH DRUIDIBEG, SOUTH UIST*
*A complex loch with many islands, Loch Druidibeg is a National*
*Nature Reserve. The sea is never far away in the Uists, and in the distance is*
*the island of Boreray, in the St Kilda group. The white sand, opposite,*
*covers long beaches to the west side of South Uist.*

*THE CUILLIN RIDGE, ISLE OF SKYE, AND LOCH ALSH*

*DUNVEGAN CASTLE, ISLE OF SKYE*

*CAMBUS O' MAY SUSPENSION BRIDGE, DEESIDE*

BALMORAL CASTLE, DEESIDE

*Completed in 1855 for Queen Victoria and Prince Albert, Balmoral
Castle is in a style known as Scottish baronial, with crowstep gables and
pepperpot turrets. It stands on the banks of the Dee, against the
backdrop of the hills and forests which characterize
Royal Deeside.*

*KILORAN BAY, ISLE OF COLONSAY*
*A haven of unspoilt peace and beauty on the north shore of this*
*small Hebridean island. The name is from Gaelic 'cill Odhrán' the cell*
*of Oran, one of the followers of St Columba.*

*ISLAY AND JURA FROM ORONSAY*
*The little island of Oronsay, just to the south of Colonsay, looks across to the*
*aptly named Paps of Jura and to the flatter lands of Islay.*

*ARDVRECK CASTLE, LOCH ASSYNT, SUTHERLAND*
*The ancient ruin of Ardvreck was the home of the Macleods of Assynt,*
*one of whom, Neil Macleod, surrendered the Marquis of Montrose to his fate*
*after his defeat in 1650 at Carbisdale, near Bonar Bridge on the east coast.*
*Opposite: Loch Assynt, one of the largest freshwater lochs of this*
*distant part of the north-west.*

*CANNA, INNER HEBRIDES*
*Along with Rum, Eigg and Muck, it is part of the Small Isles.*
*For many years the island was owned by Dr John Lorne Campbell, the Gaelic*
*folklorist, who gifted it to the National Trust for Scotland in 1981.*

*RUM FROM CANNA, INNER HEBRIDES*

*BUACHAILLE ETIVE MÒR, GLENCOE*

*BUACHAILLE ETIVE MÒR, FROM BEINN A' CHRÙLAISTE, GLENCOE*

CRAIGIEVAR CASTLE, ABERDEENSHIRE

LOCH KANAIRD, WESTER ROSS
Looking towards Ben Mòr Coigach and the Summer Isles.

*BLÀ BHEINN AND LOCH SLAPIN, ISLE OF SKYE*
*Blà Bheinn lies to the east of the main Cuillin range. The name may*
*come from Old Norse 'blá' meaning blue, along with Gaelic 'beinn' a hill.*
*Opposite: The Isle of Skye from near Applecross, across the Inner Sound.*

*ST ANDREWS, FIFE*

*In the Middle Ages St Andrews was an important ecclesiastical
and academic centre, with Scotland's oldest university, founded in 1412.
Here the enormous size of the medieval cathedral, the largest church in
Scotland, can be clearly seen. Ruins of the much older castle
stand guard above sea cliffs.*

*DUNNOTTAR CASTLE, NEAR STONEHAVEN, KINCARDINESHIRE*

*OLDSHOREMORE, SUTHERLAND*

*BADCALL BAY, SUTHERLAND*
*One of the many island-studded indentations on the north-west coast,*
*Badcall Bay is just to the south of Scourie.*

WIAY AND ULLINISH POINT, LOCH BRACADALE, ISLE OF SKYE

*The names of island, headland and loch all derive from Old Norse, a reminder of the Norse*
*occupation of these islands in the early Middle Ages.*

*THE CUILLIN HILLS AND LOCH SCAVAIG, ISLE OF SKYE*
*Gabbros and other igneous rocks form one of Scotland's finest mountain ranges.*
*The Cuillins rise dramatically from the sea, providing superb climbing*
*for the expert mountaineer.*

ABERNETHY FOREST AND MEALL A' BHUACHAILLE, STRATHSPEY

*Abernethy Forest, lying to the north of the Cairngorm mountains,*
*is one of the largest remnants of the Caledonian pine forest which once covered*
*large parts of Scotland. Within this National Nature Reserve is Loch Garten,*
*opposite, well-known for its ospreys, which were re-introduced here*
*in the 1950s, and continue to thrive.*

LOCH LINNHE

*A long inlet of the sea, Loch Linnhe stretches through*
*mountainous country from Appin, near Oban, north-eastwards to Fort William.*
*Opposite: Looking across Loch Linnhe towards Kingairloch.*

*IONA ABBEY*

*The Abbey is a modern restoration of a thirteenth-century*
*Benedictine abbey, itself built on the site of much earlier church buildings.*
*Iona has been a place of Christian sanctity since the sixth century, when Saint Columba,*
*an Irish monk, brought a Celtic form of Christianity to this part of Scotland.*
*The Iona Community was founded in 1938 to restore the buildings,*
*and has widened into other religious and social activities.*

*ST JOHN'S CROSS, IONA ABBEY*

*THE CAIRNGORM MOUNTAINS*

*LOCH PITYOULISH, STRATHSPEY*

*LOCH DUICH AND BEINN SGRITHEALL FROM STRATH CROE, WESTER ROSS*

### EILEAN DONAN CASTLE, WESTER ROSS

*A prehistoric fort here was followed by a medieval castle, long held
by the Mackenzies of Kintail. During the Jacobite rising of 1719, it was
bombarded by English warships. It sits in a commanding position at the meeting
of three sea lochs and twentieth-century restoration has made it one
of the most photographed castles in Europe.*

*LOCH SHIELDAIG, TORRIDON, WESTER ROSS*
*Shieldaig Island, at the centre of both pictures, has a fine cap of Scots pine.*
*West Highland scenery is at its best in Torridon, with changes from gloom*
*to brightness, from mist and cloud to light, creating*
*an ever-changing kaleidoscope.*

# INDEX OF PLACES